CREATE
A · STORY

A PROMPT JOURNAL TO HELP YOU WRITE A STORY

chartwell
books

EVERY STORY BEGINS WITH A SINGLE WORD.

Storytelling is as natural to us as our DNA. People from the beginning of time have been telling stories as a way to connect, entertain, and lead humanity. Our brains are literally wired to think in stories. We use narratives to explain how things work, how we make decisions, how things came to be, and even to understand who we are. Storytelling comes to us intuitively, but when it comes to writing, the mind can be its own enemy.

Create a Story is designed to help you overcome that initial writer's block and spark the creativity you were born with. Begin by selecting one of the ten genre sections. Each genre has a corresponding icon that appears at the top of each page to help you keep track of which theme you are working with. Feel free to blend genres until your heart's content or break out of your comfort zone and try genres outside the realm of what you usually write. Challenge yourself to use all of the 15-word associations or just use them to help you brainstorm the elements of your story.

Use this journal as a playground for your creativity and let your stories flow!

Write a story about:
A SPY IN THE COURT OF GENGHIS KHAN

USE THESE WORDS IN YOUR STORY:

mongol, invader, burn, expand,

horde, gold, treasure, fear, lie, tribe,

poison, magic, spirit, horses, warrior

Write a story about:

A WORLD WAR I GENERAL STUCK
IN THE TRENCHES OF THE ENEMY

USE THESE WORDS IN YOUR STORY:

blood, shell, helmet, wound, soldier, despair,

disease, hunger, ally, league, tank,

gun, draft, surrender, civilian

Write a story about:

A MAGICIAN IN THE COURT OF AN EGYPTIAN PHARAOH

USE THESE WORDS IN YOUR STORY:

snake, staff, spell, potion, trick, slave,

tyrant, race, crown, scepter,

desert, court, labor, show, survive

Write a story about:

AN ASSASSIN HIRED TO KILL THE LEGENDARY RED-BEARDED PIRATE, BARBAROSSA

USE THESE WORDS IN YOUR STORY:

ship, Mediterranean, seas, dagger,

shadow, pillage, plank, lie, loyalty,

mate, crew, murder, attack, island, shore

Write a story about:

THE SLAVE COUNCIL WHO LED THE HAITIAN REVOLUTION AGAINST FRENCH COLONISTS

USE THESE WORDS IN YOUR STORY:

liberate, shackle, prison, fight, race, blood, rebel,

freedom, family, island, wealth, power,

struggle, skin, Toussaint Louverture

Write a story about:

THE MUMMIFIER (BODY WRAPPER) IN ANCIENT EGYPT

_____

_____

_____

_____

_____

_____

_____

_____

_____

_____

_____

_____

_____

_____

_____

_____

_____

_____

_____

_____

_____

_____

USE THESE WORDS IN YOUR STORY:

death, tomb, pyramid, coffin, organ, preserve,

riches, afterlife, embalm, spirit, amulet,

bandage, King Tutankhamun, pharaoh, immortal

Write a story about:
A THIEF TRAVELING ALONG THE SILK ROAD

Write a story about:
A CHILD WHO STRIKES BIG IN THE CALIFORNIA GOLD RUSH

Write a story about:

THE ASSISTANT OF MARCO POLO

USE THESE WORDS IN YOUR STORY:

travel, world, seas, map, danger,

mongols, china, court, ship, route,

explorer, venice, rivalry, risk, fame

Write a story about:

AN ORPHAN PICKED UP ALONG THE PONY EXPRESS

Write a story about:

A PRIESTESS WHO IS KIDNAPPED BY THE VIKINGS

_____

_____

_____

_____

_____

_____

_____

_____

_____

_____

_____

_____

_____

_____

_____

_____

_____

_____

_____

_____

_____

USE THESE WORDS IN YOUR STORY:

medieval, monastery, savage, raider,

Scandinavia, homeland, pirate, seafaring, fleet, pagan,

warrior, death, pillage, voyage, realm

Write a story about:

A STOWAWAY ON THE FIRST SUBMARINE

_____
_____
_____
_____
_____
_____
_____
_____
_____
_____
_____
_____
_____
_____
_____
_____
_____
_____
_____
_____
_____
_____
_____
_____

USE THESE WORDS IN YOUR STORY:

nuclear, deep, sea, periscope, oxygen, quarters,

captain, navy, submerge, underwater,

missile, force, escape, spy, danger

Write a story about:

THE CONFIDANTE OF ALEXANDER THE GREAT

USE THESE WORDS IN YOUR STORY:

king, greece, conquer, war, expand, throne,

military, genius, empire, destroy,

miracle, oracle, gods, city, trust

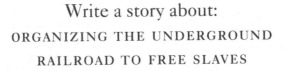

Write a story about:

ORGANIZING THE UNDERGROUND
RAILROAD TO FREE SLAVES

_____

_____

_____

_____

_____

_____

_____

_____

_____

_____

_____

_____

_____

_____

_____

_____

_____

_____

_____

_____

_____

_____

_____

USE THESE WORDS IN YOUR STORY:

freedom, escape, runaway, hideout,

secret, danger, law, shackle, track, trace, hounds,

suspicion, flee, disguise, ally

Write a story about:

A QUEEN'S TASTE-TESTER WHO IS IMMUNE TO POISON

_____
_____
_____
_____
_____
_____
_____
_____
_____
_____
_____
_____
_____
_____
_____
_____
_____
_____
_____
_____
_____
_____
_____
_____
_____

USE THESE WORDS IN YOUR STORY:

sacrifice, food, lie, deadly, bite,

assassination, plot, royalty, revolution, spy, weapon,

conspiracy, venom, choke, fear

Write a story about:

THE LIFE OF A FAMOUS PERSON WHO DIED TRAGICALLY

_____

_____

_____

_____

_____

_____

_____

_____

_____

_____

_____

_____

_____

_____

_____

_____

_____

_____

_____

_____

_____

_____

_____

USE THESE WORDS IN YOUR STORY:

crash, accident, helicopter,

drugs, fame, fan, mourn, legacy, idol, alcohol,

memorial, tattoo, shock, celebrity, life

Write a story about:

IN THE MIDST OF THE SPANISH INFLUENZA, A SCIENTIST CONDUCTS A SERIES OF UNETHICAL EXPERIMENTS TO FIND A CURE

USE THESE WORDS IN YOUR STORY:

disease, flu, pandemic, spread, virus, death,

danger, quarantine, experiment, test, vaccine,

needle, risk, guinea pig, laboratory

Write a story about:
THE WORLD'S FIRST HEART TRANSPLANT

USE THESE WORDS IN YOUR STORY:

surgeon, hospital, scalpel, experiment, nurse,

afterlife, human, organ, donor, ice,

stop, heartbeat, shock, pulse, operation

Write a story about:
BEING HUNTED DURING THE SALEM WITCH TRIALS

USE THESE WORDS IN YOUR STORY:

spell, fire, stake, accuse, judge,

townspeople, blame, hang, guilt, magic,

phobia, women, execution, colony, religion

Write a story about:

ARRIVING IN A SMALL TOWN THAT HAS A SECRET

_____
_____
_____
_____
_____
_____
_____
_____
_____
_____
_____
_____
_____
_____
_____
_____
_____
_____
_____
_____
_____
_____
_____

USE THESE WORDS IN YOUR STORY:

cult, mystery, murder, power, stranger,

newcomer, alien, weapon, silence, danger,

police, hidden, map, discovery, bond

Write a story about:
A CHILD'S ARTWORK CORRESPONDS TO A SERIES OF MURDERS IN TOWN

USE THESE WORDS IN YOUR STORY:

school, painting, disturbing, image, repulsive, insight,

clue, danger, witness, deep, understanding,

communication, help, sociopath, outlet

Write a story about:

A STRANGER SHOWS UP CLAIMING TO BE YOUR MOTHER

_____

_____

_____

_____

_____

_____

_____

_____

_____

_____

_____

_____

_____

_____

_____

_____

_____

_____

_____

_____

_____

_____

USE THESE WORDS IN YOUR STORY:

adoption, missing, abandon, blood,

lineage, genes, ghost, imposter, truth, bond,

child, relationship, secret, strings, attachment

Write a story about:

AN ART CURATOR IS ARRESTED FOR MURDER BASED OFF OF THEIR COLLECTION

USE THESE WORDS IN YOUR STORY:

artist, portray, weapon, clue, puzzle, anonymous,

witness, exhibition, collector, staged, plot, scenes,

gallery, memory, abstract

Write a story about:

A WORLD-CLASS ATHLETE MURDERED AT THE OLYMPICS

_____

_____

_____

_____

_____

_____

_____

_____

_____

_____

_____

_____

_____

_____

_____

_____

_____

_____

_____

_____

_____

_____

USE THESE WORDS IN YOUR STORY:

famous, medal, sport, rigged, place,

global, race, clue, steroid, flag,

anthem, represent, showcase, honor, choke

Write a story about:

A DETECTIVE INVESTIGATES FORTUNE TELLERS

USE THESE WORDS IN YOUR STORY:

mind, prediction, future, power, crime,

destiny, sage, voodoo, magic, spirit, whisper,

secret, tarot, divination, foresight

Write a story about:

AN AI DEVICE IS THE KEY WITNESS IN A MURDER TRIAL

USE THESE WORDS IN YOUR STORY:

technology, screen, record, pause, computer, wired,

science, machine, memory, delete, program,

encryption, failsafe, backdoor, password

Write a story about:

A COPYCAT CROOK GOES ON A STRING OF ROBBERIES THAT MIRROR FAMOUS MOVIES

Write a story about:

A SPECIAL AGENT IS CALLED ABROAD TO INVESTIGATE A STREAK OF MISSING PEOPLE

Write a story about:
A PRIVATE CATERING COMPANY SPECIALIZES IN CRIMINAL ACTIVITY

USE THESE WORDS IN YOUR STORY:

syndicate, recipe, cut, freezer, cover-up,

uniform, disguise, clean-up, crew, order,

bell, cook, burnt, raw, serve

Write a story about:

A HIGH SCHOOL PRANK GONE DEAD WRONG IS RE-LIVED DURING A CLASS REUNION

Write a story about:

A MODEL UN TEAM GOES MISSING

USE THESE WORDS IN YOUR STORY:

politics, danger, play, debate, team, represent,

rivalry, secretary, veto, vendetta, leverage,

popular, school, trip, news

Write a story about:

A DETECTIVE DISGUISES HIMSELF AS A CELEBRITY TO ENTER AN ELITE CLUB OF CRIMINALS

Write a story about:

A MECHANIC FINDS A TREASURE IN THE JUNKYARD AND IS INSTANTLY A WANTED MAN

USE THESE WORDS IN YOUR STORY:

waste, garbage, landfill, pile,

buried, sort, wreck, salvage, part, fortune,

secret, hidden, build, accident, scavenger

Write a story about:

A CYBER ATTACK HAS WIPED THE RECORDS OF THE JUSTICE DEPARTMENT

Write a story about:

AN ORPHANAGE WITH A HISTORY OF CRIMINALS

_____
_____
_____
_____
_____
_____
_____
_____
_____
_____
_____
_____
_____
_____
_____
_____
_____
_____
_____
_____
_____
_____
_____

USE THESE WORDS IN YOUR STORY:

abandon, revenge, trauma, leave, raise, gene,

lineage, training, army, league, recruit, base,

weapon, program, brainwash

Write a story about:

A YOUTUBE STAR IS KIDNAPPED ON SCREEN

_____
_____
_____
_____
_____
_____
_____
_____
_____
_____
_____
_____
_____
_____
_____
_____
_____
_____
_____
_____
_____
_____
_____

USE THESE WORDS IN YOUR STORY:

fame, fortune, screen, personality, online,

host, livestream, viral, sensation, likes,

share, ads, hostage, plea, hoax

Write a story about:

A TEACHER GETS WIND OF A BREWING SCHOOL RIVALRY THAT COULD TURN DEADLY

USE THESE WORDS IN YOUR STORY:

council, diary, gossip, teenager, mascot,

clique, bully, prank, cheat, suspend, report,

guidance, principal, truth, pressure

Write a story about:

YOUR SECRET GETS PEOPLE KILLED

Write a story about:

A COUPLE THAT HAS JUST MOVED TO A PLACE THAT ONE LOVES, AND THE OTHER HATES

USE THESE WORDS IN YOUR STORY:

travel, adventure, escape, beginning, longing, hope,

despair, mismatch, opportunity, renew, relearn,

fall, break, perspective, thrive

Write a story about:

TWO PEOPLE ARE INTRODUCED, BUT NEITHER OF THEM ADMITS HAVING MET BEFORE

Write a story about:

THE FIRST PERSON IN HISTORY TO FALL IN LOVE

USE THESE WORDS IN YOUR STORY:

prehistoric, cave, ancient, primal, danger,

survival, family, lineage, tribe, hunt, escape,

attraction, courting, mate, instinct

Write a story about:

A PERSON WHO IS GUIDED BY CUPID IN THEIR DREAMS AND STARTS A MATCHMAKING SERVICE

Write a story about:

A SOLDIER FALLS IN LOVE WITH THE DAUGHTER OF THE ENEMY

USE THESE WORDS IN YOUR STORY:

battle, combat, warrior, revenge, armor, emotion,

trust, attraction, assassin, resist, urge,

duty, honor, passion, savior

Write a story about:

THE CAR BREAKS DOWN, AND A PERSON FINDS LOVE ON THE JOURNEY TO GET A REPAIR

USE THESE WORDS IN YOUR STORY:

mechanic, hitchhike, road, rest stop,

highway, stranger, allure, attraction, metal,

engine, parts, together, rev, oil

Write a story about:

FALLING IN LOVE WITH SOMEONE WITHOUT EVER ACTUALLY MEETING FACE-TO-FACE

_____
_____
_____
_____
_____
_____
_____
_____
_____
_____
_____
_____
_____
_____
_____
_____
_____
_____
_____
_____
_____
_____
_____
_____
_____

USE THESE WORDS IN YOUR STORY:

computer, viral, camera, lens,

screen, mouse, tape, appearance, reality, stranger,

distance, touch, butterflies, save, pandemic

Write a story about:
A HUMAN FALLS FOR A JINN

Write a story about:

A COUPLE WHO SIGN AWAY THEIR SOULS ONLY TO REALIZE WHAT THEY WANTED WASN'T WORTH THE PRICE

USE THESE WORDS IN YOUR STORY:

contract, spell, bind, shackle, prisoner,

servant, hell, fire, burn, curse, angel,

fate, destiny, magic, devil

Write a story about:

AN ENCHANTED KISSING BOOTH

Write a story about:

RIVAL GANG MEMBERS FALL IN LOVE

_____
_____
_____
_____
_____
_____
_____
_____
_____
_____
_____
_____
_____
_____
_____
_____
_____
_____
_____
_____
_____
_____

USE THESE WORDS IN YOUR STORY:

street, blood, honor, respect, violence, survival,

money, drugs, attraction, accident, opposites,

enemy, bond, rebel, unite

Write a story about:

THE PERFECT PERSON, BUT THEY'RE ONLY A HOLOGRAM

_____
_____
_____
_____
_____
_____
_____
_____
_____
_____
_____
_____
_____
_____
_____
_____
_____
_____
_____
_____
_____
_____
_____

USE THESE WORDS IN YOUR STORY:

code, online, computer, robot, virtual,

reality, touch, sensation, feel, companion,

friend, listen, presence, space, time

Write a story about:

PRISON GUARD FALLS IN LOVE WITH A DEATH ROW INMATE AND BREAKS THEM OUT

_____
_____
_____
_____
_____
_____
_____
_____
_____
_____
_____
_____
_____
_____
_____
_____
_____
_____
_____
_____
_____
_____
_____

USE THESE WORDS IN YOUR STORY:

confine, shackle, duty, bars, uniform,

resist, control, obedience, last, needle,

lethal, chance, truth, escape, justice

Write a story about:

A PRINCE FALLS IN LOVE WITH HIS SERVANT

_____

_____

_____

_____

_____

_____

_____

_____

_____

_____

_____

_____

_____

_____

_____

_____

_____

_____

_____

_____

_____

_____

_____

_____

_____

_____

_____

USE THESE WORDS IN YOUR STORY:

duty, honor, service, attraction, class,

bow, realm, royalty, court, intrigue, forbidden,

scandal, stolen, corridor, punishment

Write a story about:

A SEAMSTRESS WHO CAN'T FIND A MATCH

USE THESE WORDS IN YOUR STORY:

artist, work, order, measure, type,

meddle, mingle, gossip, touch, sew,

design, ball, dress, appearance, fashion

Write a story about:
AN ASSASSIN WHO FALLS FOR THEIR TARGET

Write a story about:

AN OVERWORKED DOCTOR WHO DOESN'T HAVE TIME FOR LOVE

USE THESE WORDS IN YOUR STORY:

hospital, shift, call, sleep, patient,

surgery, schedule, match, date, connection,

prescription, burnout, scrubs, alarm, nerves

Write a story about:

AN ARTIST WHO LOST THEIR MUSE

_____
_____
_____
_____
_____
_____
_____
_____
_____
_____
_____
_____
_____
_____
_____
_____
_____
_____
_____
_____
_____
_____
_____
_____

USE THESE WORDS IN YOUR STORY:

mind, thought, dream, inspiration,

drive, satisfaction, vibrant, betrayal, fall, wander,

dervish, poet, direction, compass, soul

Write a story about:

A PERSON ATTEMPTS TO EXPERIENCE EVERY TYPE OF LOVE POSSIBLE

USE THESE WORDS IN YOUR STORY:

record, unconditional, self, playful, enduring,

romance, obsessive, mutual, platonic, familiar,

physical, emotional, mad, empathy, significant

Write a story about:
BREAKING A VALUED FAMILY TRADITION

_____
_____
_____
_____
_____
_____
_____
_____
_____
_____
_____
_____
_____
_____
_____
_____
_____
_____
_____
_____
_____
_____
_____

USE THESE WORDS IN YOUR STORY:

generation, transmit, legacy, honor,

respect, religion, culture, practice, symbol, myth,

way, belief, abandon, inherit, tribe

Write a story about:

BECOMING A PARENT UNEXPECTEDLY

Write a story about:

WRITING A LETTER THAT YOU'RE TOO AFRAID TO SEND

Write a story about:

A FRIENDSHIP THAT HAS RUN ITS COURSE

_____

_____

_____

_____

_____

_____

_____

_____

_____

_____

_____

_____

_____

_____

_____

_____

_____

_____

_____

_____

_____

_____

_____

_____

USE THESE WORDS IN YOUR STORY:

disrespect, boundary, rivalry, betrayal,

history, trust, pact, attachment, mutual,

enduring, break, envy, share, memory, outgrow

Write a story about:
EVERY FAMILY HAS A SECRET

USE THESE WORDS IN YOUR STORY:

blood, inherit, lineage, dynasty, ancestor,

belong, born, clan, tribe, descend, inbred,

tradition, history, relative, grail

Write a story about:
A SIBLING YOU THINK YOU'LL NEVER UNDERSTAND

USE THESE WORDS IN YOUR STORY:

upbringing, share, same, household,

blood, genetic, estrange, grow, twin, mutation,

complex, divergent, intuition, instinct, family

Write a story about:
CROSSING THE LINE

Write a story about:
THE FIRST DAY OF SCHOOL OR WORK

USE THESE WORDS IN YOUR STORY:

nerves, identity, perception, step, think,

debut, shine, cool, encounter, persona,

association, impression, truth, mask

Write a story about:
BEING STRANDED WITHOUT HELP

Write a story about:

FINDING A PURPOSE

_____

_____

_____

_____

_____

_____

_____

_____

_____

_____

_____

_____

_____

_____

_____

_____

_____

_____

_____

_____

_____

_____

_____

_____

_____

USE THESE WORDS IN YOUR STORY:

desire, intention, goal, aim, life,

religion, spiritual, destination, history, legacy,

reason, regret, identity, path, design

Write a story about:
DEALING WITH A PHOBIA

Write a story about:
DREAMS THAT COME TRUE

_____
_____
_____
_____
_____
_____
_____
_____
_____
_____
_____
_____
_____
_____
_____
_____
_____
_____
_____
_____
_____
_____

USE THESE WORDS IN YOUR STORY:

imagine, destiny, purpose, drive, focus,

drill, practice, advance, wish, hope,

envision, wild, belief, repress, obstacle

Write a story about:
BURYING SOMEONE YOU LOVED

USE THESE WORDS IN YOUR STORY:

despair, mourn, afterlife, regret,

inheritance, will, grieve, next, funeral,

cemetery, hole, empty, space, missing, spirit

Write a story about:

FACING CONSEQUENCES OF SOMEONE ELSE'S ACTIONS

Write a story about:
DEJA-VU... OR IS IT?

USE THESE WORDS IN YOUR STORY:

prophecy, oracle, destiny, foresight, vision,

future, see, experience, past, visit, sensation,

unthinking, predict, possibility, mind

Write a story about:
THE ALLURE OF A STRANGER

USE THESE WORDS IN YOUR STORY:

newcomer, foreigner, intrigue, danger, attraction,

mystery, curious, guest, eye, welcome,

enchant, nameless, unknown, traveler, story

Write a story about:
YOUR BIGGEST REGRET

Write a story about:
MAKING ENDS MEET

USE THESE WORDS IN YOUR STORY:

money, wealth, challenge, poverty, paycheck,

work, class, hierarchy, inheritance, success

struggle, goal, overcome, sacrifice, motivation

Write a story about:
THE BEST THING THAT EVER HAPPENED

USE THESE WORDS IN YOUR STORY:

effort, struggle, learn, win, lose, determine,

persevere, obstacle, luck, chance,

destiny, hope, mindset, help, mistake

Write a story about:

A TAXI DRIVER WHO IS HAILED BY HIS DOPPELGANGER

Write a story about:

WAKING UP IN THE BODY OF THE PERSON YOU HATE

USE THESE WORDS IN YOUR STORY:

nightmare, vision, lesson, emotion, reason, empathy,

racism, perspective, scorn, sleep, curse,

journey, enlightenment, enemy, revenge

Write a story about:

CELEBRITIES LIVING IN RETIREMENT HOMES

USE THESE WORDS IN YOUR STORY:

old, burn-out, cranky, lazy, competition, appearance,

reputation, persona, paparazzi, fame,

fan, rivalry, relationship, movie, music

Write a story about:
THE WORLD'S MOST NOTORIOUS PAPARAZZI
BECOMES A CELEBRITY

USE THESE WORDS IN YOUR STORY:

mob, blackmail, reversal, riches,

privacy, shadow, camera, fame, incentive,

accident, mirror, lens, reputation, karma, secret

Write a story about:

A PERSON WHO ACCIDENTALLY POISONS A DRUG LORD

USE THESE WORDS IN YOUR STORY:

fast food, teenager, panic, delivery,

puberty, mafia, violence, gang, profit,

ransom, hit-list, muscle, fear, accident, runaway

Write a story about:

THE TOLL BOOTH OPERATOR WHO INHERITS A FORTUNE

_____

_____

_____

_____

_____

_____

_____

_____

_____

_____

_____

_____

_____

_____

_____

_____

_____

_____

_____

_____

_____

_____

_____

_____

_____

_____

_____

USE THESE WORDS IN YOUR STORY:

coin, common, name, mundane,

routine, glass, box, cars, chance, opportunity,

will, estate, mistake, lawyer, family

Write a story about:

A BORED EMPLOYEE GETS CONTROL OF SOCIAL MEDIA ACCOUNTS OF ITS BILLION-DOLLAR COMPANY

USE THESE WORDS IN YOUR STORY:

cubicle, stapler, labels, lunchbreak, coffee,

clock, paycheck, boss, hate, scandal,

computer, power, control, password, genius

Write a story about:

A SCIENTIST ACCIDENTALLY CREATES A FRANKENSTEIN DOG HE LEARNS TO LOVE

Write a story about:
A THERAPIST FOR THERAPISTS

Write a story about:

A PICKPOCKET WHO ACCIDENTALLY ROBS A DICTATOR

Write a story about:
THE WORLD'S WORST ZOOKEEPER

USE THESE WORDS IN YOUR STORY:

animal, cage, keep, audience,

display, mask, learn, perform, entertain,

leash, whip, shovel, radio, ranger, purpose

Write a story about:

YOUR DIARY IS LEAKED AND BECOMES
A BEST-SELLING PHENOMENON

Write a story about:

THE GRIM REAPER COMES TO EARTH AND
IS CELEBRATED AS A HERO

Write a story about:
A WOMAN WHO DOESN'T KNOW SHE'S HAUNTED BY HER PETS

USE THESE WORDS IN YOUR STORY:

apartment, cat, dog, soul, spirit, ghost,

vision, imagine, mind, message,

taxidermy, death, companion, friend, direction

Write a story about:

AN ANCESTOR REMEMBERED FOR
AN INSIGNIFICANT ACT

USE THESE WORDS IN YOUR STORY:

trivial, reputation, misunderstanding, invention, discovery,

accident, namesake, embarrassment, inheritance,

identity, descendent, fame, fortune, joke, value

Write a story about:
A SUPERFAN BECOMES THEIR IDOL'S ASSISTANT

USE THESE WORDS IN YOUR STORY:

celebrity, fame, favorite, club, job,

resume, hire, reality, illusion, journey,

paycheck, service, truth, human, weakness

Write a story about:

A JUDGE ON TV GETS TAKEN TO COURT

_____

_____

_____

_____

_____

_____

_____

_____

_____

_____

_____

_____

_____

_____

_____

_____

_____

_____

_____

_____

_____

_____

_____

_____

USE THESE WORDS IN YOUR STORY:

crime, celebrity, justice, jury, camera, tabloid,

network, revenge, lawyer, accusation,

jail, bail, evidence, series, mirror

Write a story about:

A PERSON WHO THINKS EVERYTHING IS A CONTEST

_____

_____

_____

_____

_____

_____

_____

_____

_____

_____

_____

_____

_____

_____

_____

_____

_____

_____

_____

_____

_____

_____

USE THESE WORDS IN YOUR STORY:

competative, race, win, lose, strategy, angle,

motivation, preparation, analysis, target, weakness,

growth, assessment, aim, execution

Write a story about:
THE MOST RIDICULOUS NIGHT EVER

USE THESE WORDS IN YOUR STORY:

absurd, nonsense, dawn, whim, vanity,

extravagant, invitation, odyssey, party, mission,

obstacle, unbelievable, accident, trouble, impossible

Write a story about:
THE DEMON WHO'S AFRAID OF YOU

USE THESE WORDS IN YOUR STORY:

satan, angel, hell, punishment, shadow, insignificant,

fire, whimper, haunt, negotiate,

timid, reluctant, conscience, small, conjure

Write a story about:
A CENTURIES-OLD INFORMATION NETWORK
RUN BY VAMPIRES

USE THESE WORDS IN YOUR STORY:

blood, fangs, coffin, lure, secrets,

ancient, crypt, price, control, power,

dynasty, fence, darkness, suck, Dracula

Write a story about:

A LIBRARIAN COMES ACROSS A BOOK OF SPELLS

Write a story about:

SOMEONE FINDS A MAGIC CLOAK
LEFT AT A LAUNDROMAT

_____
_____
_____
_____
_____
_____
_____
_____
_____
_____
_____
_____
_____
_____
_____
_____
_____
_____
_____
_____
_____
_____
_____
_____

USE THESE WORDS IN YOUR STORY:

fold, clothes, steam, pocket, return, cover,

customer, wash, dry, invisible, veil, hood,

sorcery, magician, abandoned, enchantment

Write a story about:

WAKING UP IN A PARALLEL WORLD AFTER AN ACCIDENT

USE THESE WORDS IN YOUR STORY:

helix, sign, amnesia, curse, drug, evolution,

portal, tunnel, optical, illusion,

magic, travel, magnet, electric, duplicate

Write a story about:

AN ANTIQUE SHOP OWNER DISCOVERS
A CURSED MEDALLION

_____
_____
_____
_____
_____
_____
_____
_____
_____
_____
_____
_____
_____
_____
_____
_____
_____
_____
_____
_____
_____
_____

USE THESE WORDS IN YOUR STORY:

dealer, chipped, time, history, bric-a-brac,

possessed, power, wake, spirit, specialty,

value, enslavement, relic, collection, rare

Write a story about:

A RUNAWAY OGRE PRINCESS

_____

_____

_____

_____

_____

_____

_____

_____

_____

_____

_____

_____

_____

_____

_____

_____

_____

_____

_____

_____

_____

_____

_____

USE THESE WORDS IN YOUR STORY:

demon, damsel, fire, dynasty, hunt,

secret, verse, phantom, palace,

clay, quest, beast, bird, prison, conceal

Write a story about:

BEING LOST ON A HIKE AND FINDING THE ANCIENT TREE OF LIFE

USE THESE WORDS IN YOUR STORY:

roots, source, elixir, exude, veil,

forest, search, lure, mystical, flower,

forbidden, creature, magic, ancient, tangle

Write a story about:

A PERSON BUYS A CHAIR FROM A GARAGE SALE THAT TRANSFORMS INTO THE THRONE OF A TYRANT KING

USE THESE WORDS IN YOUR STORY:

shed, relic, antique, portal, key, reign,

overlord, shapeshift, corruption,

appearance, vanish, seize, topple, rule, junk

Write a story about:
A KEEPER OF MAGIC BEES

Write a story about:
A CHARACTER BUYS A HOUSE SURROUNDED BY A FOREST OF TALKING TREES

Write a story about:

A GIRL HITS PUBERTY AND IS REBORN AN ORACLE

USE THESE WORDS IN YOUR STORY:

period, mature, stage, growth, phase, cycle,

seer, premonition, stars, vision, horoscope,

prophecy, dream, birth, blossom

Write a story about:

AN AMATEUR FILMMAKER ACCIDENTALLY PREDICTS THE FUTURE THROUGH HIS FILM

Write a story about:
A CHILDHOOD MYTH THAT TURNS OUT TO BE TRUE

USE THESE WORDS IN YOUR STORY:

story, fable, tale, family, truth, secret, creature,

nightmare, monster, telling, listen,

thread, lineage, folklore, legend

Write a story about:

A MUSICIAN THAT CAN BRING BACK THE DEAD
WITH THEIR MUSIC

Write a story about:
MINERS FIND A MAGICAL RACE BENEATH THE EARTH'S SURFACE

USE THESE WORDS IN YOUR STORY:

hammer, shovel, gravel, canary, tunnel,

landfall, myth, creature, unprecedented, fossil,

monster, level, underground, world, light

Write a story about:

AN INHERITED COIN COLLECTION TRANSPORTS
YOU TO DIFFERENT WORLDS

Write a story about:

A TATTOO ARTIST WITH CURSED INK

USE THESE WORDS IN YOUR STORY:

needle, bleed, color, sign, design, mistake, fade,

remove, canvas, body, eternity,

bond, spell, unleash, magic

Write a story about:

A DAY IN THE LIFE OF THE VOODOO QUEEN

USE THESE WORDS IN YOUR STORY:

royalty, shaman, curse, vow, amulet, conjure,

spell, ritual, cult, underground, folk,

sorcerer, resurrect, charm, deity

Write a story about:

A WITCH WHO MUST FORFEIT HER POWERS, BUT THE SPELL GOES WRONG

USE THESE WORDS IN YOUR STORY:

magic, cauldron, scarecrow, bonfire, wicked, broom,

charm, wiccan, contract, bind, mistake,

trial, wand, contract, punish

Write a story about:

A PERSON WORKING IN A SALT FACTORY FALLS INTO THE WASTE PILE AND ENDS UP IN A DESERT KINGDOM

USE THESE WORDS IN YOUR STORY:

sand, sea, mirage, genie, assassin, tribe,

caravan, camel, tent, machine, mystery,

portal, gateway, purgatory, pepper

Write a story about:

A BILLIONAIRE HOSTS A SERIES OF CONTESTS IN ORDER TO CHOOSE A WORTHY SUCCESSOR

_____

_____

_____

_____

_____

_____

_____

_____

_____

_____

_____

_____

_____

_____

_____

_____

_____

_____

_____

_____

_____

_____

USE THESE WORDS IN YOUR STORY:

money, prize, race, compete, rival, cutthroat,

entertainment, peasant, gladiator, survive,

bowl, kill, future, heir, conglomerate

Write a story about:

A DIVER UNCOVERS GOVERNMENT SECRETS BURIED AT THE BOTTOM OF THE OCEAN

_____

_____

_____

_____

_____

_____

_____

_____

_____

_____

_____

_____

_____

_____

_____

_____

_____

_____

_____

_____

_____

_____

_____

USE THESE WORDS IN YOUR STORY:

water, coast, mask, oxygen, pressure, tank,

boat, vast, space, tied, lifeline, box,

redacted, leak, limit

Write a story about:

AN INMATE GRANTED CLEMENCY TO FIGHT RAGING WILDFIRES

USE THESE WORDS IN YOUR STORY:

chance, freedom, opportunity, flame, burn,

desert, rage, shackles, sacrifice,

execution, mercy, sentence, plea, justice, repent

Write a story about:

A GROUP OF SURVIVORS TAKE A CROSS-COUNTRY TRIP IN THE AFTERMATH OF WAR

_____
_____
_____
_____
_____
_____
_____
_____
_____
_____
_____
_____
_____
_____
_____
_____
_____
_____
_____
_____
_____
_____
_____

USE THESE WORDS IN YOUR STORY:

trauma, leftovers, last, remains, skeleton, wreck,

massacre, salvage, picking, overrun, road,

path, journey, hope, beginning

Write a story about:
THE RISE OF A MARTIAL ARTS GURU WITH A SECRET MISSION

_____

_____

_____

_____

_____

_____

_____

_____

_____

_____

_____

_____

_____

_____

_____

_____

_____

_____

_____

_____

_____

_____

USE THESE WORDS IN YOUR STORY:

athlete, discipline, kick, punch, focus, mind, system,

warfare, enemy, master, bear,

skill, silent, aim, ladder

Write a story about:

A BLACK-MARKET ORGAN DEALER WHO WANTS OUT

Write a story about:

AFTER HISTORY'S LARGEST EARTHQUAKE, A PERSON FINDS THEMSELVES TRAPPED UNDERGROUND

USE THESE WORDS IN YOUR STORY:

plate, shift, shake, crack, magma, fire,

shatter, snap, cover, debris, destruction,

crush, weight, richter, fault

Write a story about:

A TEENAGER WHO BECOMES THE SOLE WITNESS OF A MASSACRE

USE THESE WORDS IN YOUR STORY:

adolescence, school, camera, tape, eye, peep,

hideout, party, drink, drama, protection,

bully, weapon, violence, warning

Write a story about:

A COLLEGE STUDENT WHO ACCIDENTALLY
JOINS A DANGEROUS CULT

_____
_____
_____
_____
_____
_____
_____
_____
_____
_____
_____
_____
_____
_____
_____
_____
_____
_____
_____
_____
_____
_____
_____
_____
_____

USE THESE WORDS IN YOUR STORY:

sorority, frat, paddle, initiation, longing,

conscript, house, roommate, clique,

new, guru, charisma, follow, blind, loyalty

Write a story about:

A MORTICIAN WHO WORKS FOR THE MOB TO COVER UP MURDER

USE THESE WORDS IN YOUR STORY:

undertaker, death, coffin, parting, farewell, grave,

business, funeral, shroud, burn,

secret, crypt, tomb, mummy, hide

Write a story about:

A VILLAGE FISHERMAN WHO MUST SAVE HIS FAMILY FROM A RAIDING PARTY OF PIRATES

USE THESE WORDS IN YOUR STORY:

boat, water, sustenance, labor, pearl, catch,

fish, attack, invasion, seize, shackle,

bound, tear, suppress, service

Write a story about:

A REPORTER GETS A LIST OF OFFICIALS RUNNING THE CRIMINAL UNDERWORLD FROM AN ANONYMOUS SOURCE

USE THESE WORDS IN YOUR STORY:

air, script, camera, truth, present, audience,

headline, package, shoot, guilt, profile,

risk, trafficking, systemic, whistleblower

Write a story about:

A NEWS MOGUL OPERATING TO HIDE THE TRUTH

USE THESE WORDS IN YOUR STORY:

empire, money, stakes, stocks,

projection, investor, reputation, lie, coverup,

bury, information, leak, story, lineup, secret

Write a story about:

A SCIENTIST IS HUNTED BY THE ENEMY STATE TRYING TO BURY THEIR WORLD-CHANGING DISCOVERIES

Write a story about:

A CHILD PRODIGY BECOMES
WORLD FAMOUS FOR HIS ART

Write a story about:

A PERSON WINS THE LOTTERY, ONLY TO DISCOVER IT WAS RIGGED AS A PLOT TO FRAME THEM FOR MURDER

USE THESE WORDS IN YOUR STORY:

jackpot, lucky, number, draw, ticket, setup,

conspiracy, fame, fortune, limelight, accuse,

suspect, calculation, unravel, cover

Write a story about:

A TOYMAKER DISCOVERS HIS COMPANY IS SOLD TO CRIMINALS WITH NEFARIOUS PLANS FOR HIS TOYS

USE THESE WORDS IN YOUR STORY:

machine, factory, tinker, novelty, collection,

production, violence, defile, abomination, evil,

franchise, distribute, coverup, abuse, plant

Write a story about:

A PROGRAMMER FOR THE CIA SPARKS A REBELLION

_____

_____

_____

_____

_____

_____

_____

_____

_____

_____

_____

_____

_____

_____

_____

_____

_____

_____

_____

_____

_____

_____

_____

_____

USE THESE WORDS IN YOUR STORY:

computer, code, binary, password, surveillance,

plant, virus, hack, invade, inspire,

revolution, social, experiment, meddle, target

Write a story about:

A SUBWAY ARCHITECT UNCOVERS AN UNDERWORLD

USE THESE WORDS IN YOUR STORY:

track, line, train, headlight, fog, crash,

control, conductor, map, tunnel,

derail, shadow, beast, lost, grime

Write a story about:

A JUDGE FOR THE INTERNATIONAL CRIMINAL COURT FINDS THEIR NAME ON A HIT LIST

Write a story about:

SIBLINGS WHO DISCOVER THEIR PARENTS ARE NOTORIOUS INTERNATIONAL CRIME BOSSES

Write a story about:

A SERIAL KILLER WHO WENT DORMANT

_____

_____

_____

_____

_____

_____

_____

_____

_____

_____

_____

_____

_____

_____

_____

_____

_____

_____

_____

_____

_____

_____

_____

_____

_____

USE THESE WORDS IN YOUR STORY:

enemy, love, criminal, gruesome,

victim, duty, morals, relationship, secrets,

marriage, murder, criminal, passion, dilemma

Write a story about:

A CREATURE WHO BECOMES MORE HUMAN WITH EVERY PERSON HE KILLS

Write a story about:

AN IDOL APPEARS ON YOUR FRONT DOOR WITH REAL HUMAN BODY PARTS

USE THESE WORDS IN YOUR STORY:

ritual, magic, exorcism, doom, leather, ceremony, blood,

seance, atonement, order, tradition,

worship, embodiment, deity, sacrifice

Write a story about:

A PERSON WAKES UP WITH A FADING REFLECTION

USE THESE WORDS IN YOUR STORY:

mirror, gone, vanish, connection, bargain, freedom,

stolen, demon, curse, haunt, identity,

lost, time, darkness, shadow

Write a story about:
A DIARY THAT PREDICTS PEOPLE'S DEATHS

Write a story about:

A DEAD LOVED ONE RETURNS WITH A WARNING

USE THESE WORDS IN YOUR STORY:

departed, seance, grief, message, divide,

afterlife, grave, haunt, crossing,

realm, hallucination, wisp, vision, daze, soul

Write a story about:

A BILLIONAIRE DIVER KEEPS POOLS OF DEAD BODIES

_____
_____
_____
_____
_____
_____
_____
_____
_____
_____
_____
_____
_____
_____
_____
_____
_____
_____
_____
_____
_____
_____
_____
_____
_____

USE THESE WORDS IN YOUR STORY:

estate, company, entertainment, reproach, psychopath,

sociopath, lure, victim, seal, hook,

game, bloat, money, mind, underwater

Write a story about:

A VENTRILOQUIST WHOSE PUPPETS ARE MADE FROM REAL BODIES

USE THESE WORDS IN YOUR STORY:

strings, dance, pull, macabre, sideshow, control,

cannibal, hunt, lure, puppeteer,

doll, stitch, skin, stench, stage

Write a story about:

A MANNEQUIN SALESMAN HAS A STORE FULL OF REAL MONSTERS

USE THESE WORDS IN YOUR STORY:

display, storage, display, hideout, underworld,

creep, mask, beware, entry, Halloween,

body, model, dominion, design, fake

Write a story about:

A CURSED SORCERER IS ACCIDENTALLY
FREED AND WREAKS HAVOC

USE THESE WORDS IN YOUR STORY:

spirit, fire, magic, curse, ring, escape,

vengeance, wrath, power, destroy, divide,

veil, ego, foolish, spell

Write a story about:

A CHILD'S IMAGINARY FRIEND TURNS OUT TO BE A SERIAL KILLER

USE THESE WORDS IN YOUR STORY:

ghost, memory, belief, mind, play, innocence, violate,

shadow, vision, mate, pretend, fake,

dream, reality, weapon

Write a story about:

A CHEF WHO COOKS WITH HUMAN FLESH

USE THESE WORDS IN YOUR STORY:

kitchen, service, waiter, restaurant,

cannibal, poison, serial, axe, chop, hack,

freezer, deranged, monster, taste, teeth

Write a story about:

A CLUB INITIATION REQUIRING BODILY HARM

Write a story about:

A MAD SCIENTIST WHO CONTROLS
AN ASYLUM OF AXE MURDERS

USE THESE WORDS IN YOUR STORY:

experiment, operation, demon, hell, fire,

jail, blood, guts, mind, realm, power,

illusion, force, psyche, chain

Write a story about:

AFTER A SURGERY, THE PATIENT EXPERIENCES MEMORIES OF MURDER

USE THESE WORDS IN YOUR STORY:

scalpel, operation, mix-up, transplant, oxygen,

pulse, shock, transfusion, nurse,

code, afterlife, rebirth, mind, unlock, chamber

Write a story about:

A MONSTER WHO LURES VICTIMS WITH SOUNDS OF A CRYING BABY

USE THESE WORDS IN YOUR STORY:

forest, trail, hunt, seek, prey, smell, bait,

empathy, darkness, scales, voice,

memory, fear, mistake, instinct

Write a story about:

A PSYCHIATRIST WHO TURNS OUT TO BE
A WITCH DOCTOR

Write a story about:
NIGHTMARES COME TO LIFE

USE THESE WORDS IN YOUR STORY:

slumber, door, deep, REM, alarm, access,

impossible, possession, boogeyman, curse,

conduit, creature, underworld, closet, passage

Write a story about:

A PERSON WAKES UP EVERY DAY EXPERIENCING
A NEW DEATH

USE THESE WORDS IN YOUR STORY:

dream, reality, imagination, loop, control, vision,

undone, choice, plague, stars, disquieted,

grisly, spell, inheritance, pain

Write a story about:

AN ARCHAEOLOGIST ACCIDENTALLY UNLEASHES AN ANCIENT CURSE DURING AN EXCAVATION

Write a story about:

A NEIGHBOR WHO GIVES OUT
BODY PARTS FOR HALLOWEEN

USE THESE WORDS IN YOUR STORY:

costume, trick, treat, children,

candy, route, house, visit, poison, kill,

monster, reaper, witchcraft, piece, meat

Write a story about:

A SLOWLY DETERIORATING BODY THAT CAN ONLY BE SAVED BY CONTINUOUSLY REPLACING ORGANS WITH THE STOLEN ORGANS OF OTHERS

USE THESE WORDS IN YOUR STORY:

body, decay, organs, kidneys, lungs, heart,

limbs, monster, killer, surgery, undead,

thief, immortal, crime, grave, morgue

Write a story about:

A SLEEP PARALYSIS DEMON THAT'S FORCED TO WATCH HUMANS PLAGUED BY DEMONIC POSSESSIONS THEY SLEEP

Write a story about:

A MURDERER BREAKS OUT FROM
A VIRTUAL-REALITY PRISON

USE THESE WORDS IN YOUR STORY:

criminal, mind, escape, hack, plot, map,

control, lock, key, maze, virus,

consciousness, barrier, guard, alarm

Write a story about:

A PERSON WASHED UP ON A REMOTE ISLAND AND DISCOVERS
A SECRET CIVILIZATION OF HIGHLY EVOLVED PEOPLE

USE THESE WORDS IN YOUR STORY:

shore, isolated, mirage, inhabit, shipwreck, tide,

anchor, disconnected, contact, evolution,

adapt, incubator, hubris, timeless, species

Write a story about:

A TEENAGER DISCOVERS THE POWER TO HEAR PEOPLE'S THOUGHTS BY TOUCHING THEM

USE THESE WORDS IN YOUR STORY:

adolescent, hormones, awakening, physical, stage, growth,

mature, perception, sense, experiment,

mutation, unlock, cost, family, secret

Write a story about:

GROWING A BABY IN THE GARDEN

USE THESE WORDS IN YOUR STORY:

seed, egg, fertilization, honey, polination, soil,

roots, splice, selection, harvest,

plant, future, science, experiment, evolution

Write a story about:

AN ASTRONAUT LOST AT SPACE DISCOVERS
A LIFE-SAVING PARASITE

USE THESE WORDS IN YOUR STORY:

ship, stellar, guise, symbiotic, system, cosmos,

asteroid, germinate, vaccine, orbit,

mission, atmosphere, alien, galaxy, hole

Write a story about:

A TRAPPED HYPNOTIST MUST FIGHT A WAY OUT OF THEIR OWN MIND

USE THESE WORDS IN YOUR STORY:

pendulum, hallucination, slumber, control, zombie,

repressed, unconscious, sense, waking, inner,

lock, memory, prison, escape, coma

Write a story about:

A PERSON GETS AN EYE TRANSPLANT AND CAN NOW SEE THE FUTURE

USE THESE WORDS IN YOUR STORY:

sight, cornea, gift, donor, witchcraft, horoscope,

sky, stars, sense, awaken, recovery,

consequence, blind, psychic, mystic

Write a story about:

A STUNTMAN INJURED ON SET WAKES
UP WITH THE POWER TO FLY

USE THESE WORDS IN YOUR STORY:

hoax, circus, film, accident, injury,

performer, showman, stage, amputation,

surgery, dive, bird, train, set, therapy

Write a story about:

A MISSING PERSON RETURNS AFTER 20 YEARS WITH THE POWER TO MOVE THINGS WITH HIS MIND

_____
_____
_____
_____
_____
_____
_____
_____
_____
_____
_____
_____
_____
_____
_____
_____
_____
_____
_____
_____
_____
_____
_____
_____

USE THESE WORDS IN YOUR STORY:

disappearance, vanish, skeleton, runaway, search,

unidentified, trace, clue, paranormal, telekinesis,

power, cover-up, agent, clandestine, past

Write a story about:

A RADIOACTIVE FLOWER BEGINS SPREADING ON EARTH

_____

_____

_____

_____

_____

_____

_____

_____

_____

_____

_____

_____

_____

_____

_____

_____

_____

_____

_____

_____

_____

_____

_____

USE THESE WORDS IN YOUR STORY:

pollution, toxin, radiation, mutation, lab, alter,

deform, pollen, growth, seedling, engineered,

modified, nuclear, emission, airborne

Write a story about:

A CITY PLANNER IS CONTRACTED TO BUILD THE FIRST COLONY ON THE MOON

USE THESE WORDS IN YOUR STORY:

crater, urban, nest, map, corporation, space,

galaxy, gravity, risk, emigration, orbit,

eclipse, shadow, creature, unexpected

Write a story about:

GLOBAL WARMING MELTS A GLACIER AND WAKES
A FROZEN ANCIENT PREDATOR

Write a story about:
THE SUN BEGINS TO DIE

USE THESE WORDS IN YOUR STORY:

star, flare, burn, spark, fizzle, black,

darkness, collapse, dwarf, hole, galaxy,

explosion, glare, zenith, apocalypse

Write a story about:

A BLACK HOLE SWALLOWS EARTH'S SOLAR SYSTEM AND BLENDS PAST, PRESENT, AND FUTURE TIMELINES

Write a story about:

A SERIES OF ECLIPSES TRIGGERS A STRANGE
GENE ACTIVATION IN THE WORLD

USE THESE WORDS IN YOUR STORY:

astronomy, moon, sun, shadow, star, radiation,

transformation, DNA, binary, variable, code,

suppress, viral, response, trait

Write a story about:

FOOD FILLED WITH MICROCHIPS IS GROWN TO CONTROL POPULATIONS

USE THESE WORDS IN YOUR STORY:

additives, organic, implant, sequence, mind, conspiracy,

activate, track, registry, laboratory,

detect, matrix, monitor, signature, revolution

Write a story about:
MIND TRANSFER IS NOW
A COMMODITY FOR SALE

USE THESE WORDS IN YOUR STORY:

chip, download, product, memory, exchange,

erase, fail, history, forget, wipe, save,

soul, robot, virus, corrupted

Write a story about:

GENE EDITING CREATES A NEW SOCIAL HIERARCHY

Write a story about:

THE WILL OF A BILLIONAIRE DEMANDS
ITS ROBOT ASSISTANT'S MEMORY BE ERASED

USE THESE WORDS IN YOUR STORY:

inheritance, order, trust, bequeath, heir,

instructions, secret, legacy, intention, money, wealth,

witness, crime, empire, collapse

Write a story about:

AN UNCONTACTED TRIBE COMMUNICATES
WITH A HIVE MIND

USE THESE WORDS IN YOUR STORY:

native, isolate, immunity, survival, danger,

curiosity, link, bee, nest, queen,

worker, hierarchy, gold, presence, swarm

Write a story about:

AN ISOLATED TOWN IN THE ALPS GETS A NEW SHERIFF

USE THESE WORDS IN YOUR STORY:

snow, mountain, peak, hook, noose, rope,

frostbite, wolves, patrol, subzero, temperature,

summit, climb, outlaw, outsider

Write a story about:
THE TUNDRA BECOMES THE NEW HOTSPOT
FOR CRIMINALS

Write a story about:

A GOLD RUSH IN THE SAHARA DESERT

USE THESE WORDS IN YOUR STORY:

Africa, sand, dune, nomadic, border,

dispute, lawless, wild, sparse,

oasis, treasure, hunt, dust, barren, luck

Write a story about:

VIGILANTE JUSTICE SERVED IN A COUNTRY-TOWN CONTROLLED BY A SINGLE FAMILY

USE THESE WORDS IN YOUR STORY:

watchman, loyalty, supporter, mask, defend, corruption,

control, grip, bought, jail, unlimited,

escape, bandit, jurisdiction, rogue

Write a story about:

A CARAVAN OF RICHES IS SURROUNDED BY BANDITS NOT INTERESTED IN ITS GOODS

USE THESE WORDS IN YOUR STORY:

desert, kingdom, route, passage, toll,

highwaymen, assassin, loot, stickup, camel,

horse, weapon, information, treasure, plot

Write a story about:
A NATURAL DISASTER LEAVES A GROUP OF MINERS STRANDED IN HOSTILE TERRITORY

USE THESE WORDS IN YOUR STORY:

hurricane, cyclone, earthquake, tsunami, blast,

destruction, landfall, mudslide, trapped,

underground, unstable, mercy, foreigner, misfortune, enemy

Write a story about:

A FARMING TOWN IS HIRED TO GROW A SECRET CROP

USE THESE WORDS IN YOUR STORY:

country, plain, field, empty, desolate, nondisclosure,

agreement, isolated, clueless, contain,

information, seed, control, domination, monopoly

Write a story about:

A CYBER ATTACK DRAINS THE WORLD BANK

_____

_____

_____

_____

_____

_____

_____

_____

_____

_____

_____

_____

_____

_____

_____

_____

_____

_____

_____

_____

_____

_____

_____

_____

USE THESE WORDS IN YOUR STORY:

computer, leak, invade, cryptic, formula,

unknown, drain, robbery, vigilante, territory, control,

virus, infect, hardware, delete

Write a story about:

A GROUP OF RANCHERS IS HIRED TO TAME
A SCIENTIFICALLY ENGINEERED BEAST

Write a story about:

RAIDERS THREATEN YOUR HOMELAND

_____

_____

_____

_____

_____

_____

_____

_____

_____

_____

_____

_____

_____

_____

_____

_____

_____

_____

_____

_____

_____

_____

USE THESE WORDS IN YOUR STORY:

invasion, alien, monster, creep, surprise, attack,

ferocious, ruthless, blitzkrieg, level,

submit, enemy, savior, order, survive

Write a story about:

A HIDDEN SOCIETY IS FORCED TO REVEAL ITSELF TO THE REST OF THE WORLD

USE THESE WORDS IN YOUR STORY:

expose, cellar, cave, veiled, bunker, doomsday,

ultimatum, leverage, politics, survival, antics,

display, hostage, mercy, solution

Write a story about:

A REPLACEMENT GOVERNMENT MUST UNCOVER THE TOWN LORE TO SURVIVE

Write a story about:

A MATRIARCH LEADS A REVOLUTION AGAINST INVADERS

USE THESE WORDS IN YOUR STORY:

woman, queen, princess, witch, angel,

enemy, plot, mother, crest, tribe, family,

lineage, birth, rule, strategy

Write a story about:
A HACKER ACCIDENTALLY ENTERS A NEW REALM OF THREATENING CYBERSPACE

Write a story about:
THE OUTPOST DISCOVERS AN UNEXPECTED ENEMY

USE THESE WORDS IN YOUR STORY:

outlying, stronghold, settlement, patrol,

tent, remote, frontier, scan, battalion, lookout,

watchtower, wall, creature, encroach, alarm

Write a story about:

A REALITY SHOW GONE BAD LEAVES A PERSON STRANDED IN THE MIDDLE OF A TRIBAL FEUD

host, game, question, bell, risk, wager negotiate,

camera, blackout, extortion, leverage,

pawn, head, blackmail, warrior

Write a story about:

A DETOUR IN THE ROAD LEADS A PERSON TO UNKNOWN TERRITORY

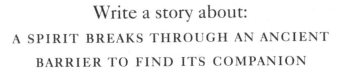

Write a story about:

A SPIRIT BREAKS THROUGH AN ANCIENT
BARRIER TO FIND ITS COMPANION

USE THESE WORDS IN YOUR STORY:

tether, unlock, talisman, boundary,

violation, cosmic, order, balance, undo,

history, abomination, reaper, chase, fugitive

Write a story about:
A VILLAGE TAKES SHIFTS GUARDING THE CEMETERY TO HIDE SOMETHING

USE THESE WORDS IN YOUR STORY:

seclusion, privy, knowledge, secret, sanctuary,

reputation, recruit, dead, spirit, creature,

treaty, mausoleum, project, lethal, protect

Write a story about:

HIRED GUARDS PROTECTING THE MYSTERIOUS FOREST ARE PICKED OFF ONE-BY-ONE

USE THESE WORDS IN YOUR STORY:

gate, entrance, border, boundary, kill,

shadow, death, unknown, mystery, frontier,

lawless, rule, challenge, face-off, smoke

Inspiring | Educating | Creating | Entertaining

Brimming with creative inspiration, how-to
projects, and useful information to enrich your
everyday life, quarto.com is a favorite destination
for those pursuing their interests and passions.

First published in 2021 by Chartwell Books, an imprint of The Quarto Group,
142 West 36th Street, 4th Floor, New York, NY 10018, USA
T (212) 779-4972 F (212) 779-6058 www.Quarto.com

Chartwell titles are also available at discount for retail, wholesale, promotional, and bulk purchase. For details, contact the Special Sales
Manager by email at specialsales@quarto.com or by mail at The Quarto Group, Attn: Special Sales Manager, 100 Cummings Center Suite
265D, Beverly, MA 01915 USA.

10 9 8 7 6

ISBN: 978-0-7858-3926-2

Publisher: Rage Kindelsperger
Creative Director: Laura Drew
Managing Editor: Cara Donaldson
Project Editor: Leeann Moreau
Editorial Assistants: Alma Gomez Martinez and Yashu Perichurla
Text: Sarosh Arif
Cover and Interior Design: Beth Middleworth

Printed in China